Horses

Elsie Nelley

Contents

What Horses Look Like

Horses are animals.

Some horses are big.

Some horses are small.

A horse has a big head and a long neck.

A horse has long legs and a long tail, too.

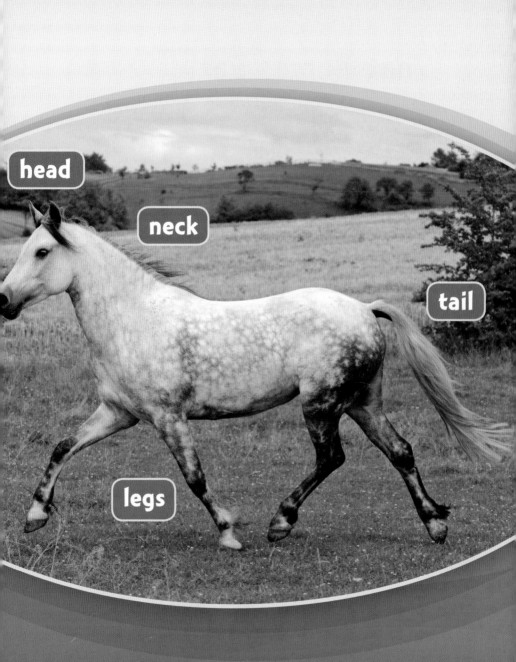

head

neck

tail

legs

What Horses Eat

Horses eat grass and **hay**.
They eat carrots
and apples, too.

They drink lots of water.

A baby horse is a **foal**.

A foal drinks milk
from its mother.

Where Horses Live

Lots of horses live outside on farms.

Some horses live in big sheds on farms if it is cold.

What Horses Can Do

Some horses

can run very fast.

They win races.

Some horses jump
over fences at a show.

Children like to ride horses.

They can ride horses

on a farm or a beach.

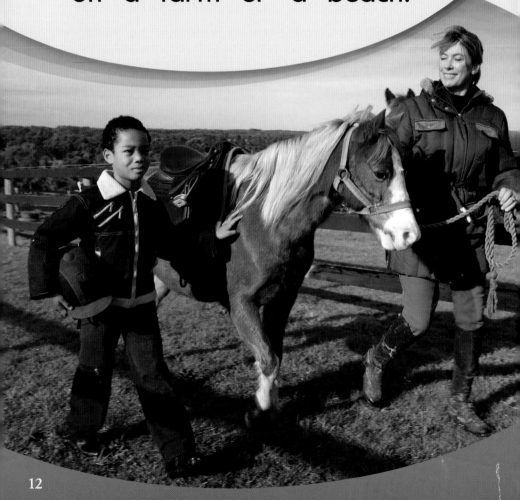

Some children go
to a **riding school**.
They have lots of fun
going over the jumps.

Horses can walk
for a long time
with heavy bags.

They are work horses.

Horses are animals
that help us.

Glossary

foal

hay

riding school